My Pet

Ferrets

My Pet Ferrets

by **Amy Gelman**
photographs by **Andy King**

All About Pets

Lerner Publications Company • Minneapolis

To Tim, Sophie, and Diane—A.G.

Acknowledgments:

The author would like to thank the Kelly family, especially Claudia and Erin Kelly, for their patience and enthusiasm. Thanks also to Pamela Greene of Ferret Central.

Additional photos courtesy of: © Ted Levin/Animals Animals, p. 13 (upper right); © Peter Weimann/Animals Animals, p. 13 (lower left); © Beth Davidow, p. 13 (upper left and lower right), 17, 19, 21; © Renee Stockdale/Animals Animals, pp. 16, 47 (lower right), 52, 53, 54; Patricia A. Musick/Treasured Ferrets, p. 27; Jim Simondet/Independent Picture Service, p. 30 (upper left, middle, center right); Andy King, p. 30 (upper right, lower right); © Rachel Giese, p. 41; Patricia Asheuer, p. 47 (upper left); Nancy Smedstad-Koons/Independent Picture Service, p. 58 (both).

Lerner Publications Company
A division of Lerner Publishing Group
241 First Avenue North
Minneapolis, Minnesota 55401 U.S.A.

Website address: www.lernerbooks.com

Library of Congress Cataloging-in-Publication Data

Gelman, Amy, 1961–
    My pet ferrets / by Amy Gelman : photographs by Andy King.
        p.   cm. — (All about pets)
    Includes bibliographical references and index.
    Summary: Follows an eleven-year-old girl through the experience of choosing and caring for two pet ferrets; includes information about their physical characteristics, behaviors, health requirements, and associated costs.
    ISBN 0-8225-2264-0
    1. Ferrets as pets—Juvenile literature. [1. Ferrets. 2. Pets.] I. King,
Andy, ill. II. Title. III. Series
SF459.F47.G45   2001
636.9'76628—dc21   99–006865

Manufactured in the United States of America
1 2 3 4 5 6 – JR – 06 05 04 03 02 01

Contents

Two ferrets would be more fun . . .

I love watching my ferrets play in their favorite toy. I call it the ferret tube.

Not too long ago, I didn't know what a ferret was. I didn't even know what one looked like. That was before I adopted two of them as pets. Lots of people don't know about ferrets—what kind of animals they are, whether they make good pets, or where to get one. But most people who meet one fall in love with them right away, just like I did. And like me, some decide they just have to have a ferret . . . or two . . . or more.

My whole family loves animals, so I had a feeling they would like having ferrets along with all our other pets.

My name is Erin Kelly. I'm 11 now, and I got my ferrets when I was 10. Their names are Snickers and Skittles, and they're both females. Having ferrets is like living with furry, playful clowns. My ferrets make me laugh at least once a day.

My family has always had pets. We have two cats named Jane and Michael. We've also had rabbits, llamas, and some ducks. Luckily, we live in the country, so there's lots of room for all those animals.

The first time I saw ferrets was at a pet store. I was looking around while my mother was buying cat food. One cage had a bunch of long, skinny animals with pointed faces and bright eyes. They were all in a furry heap, and they looked so cute!

One ferret at the pet store got a ride in an apron.

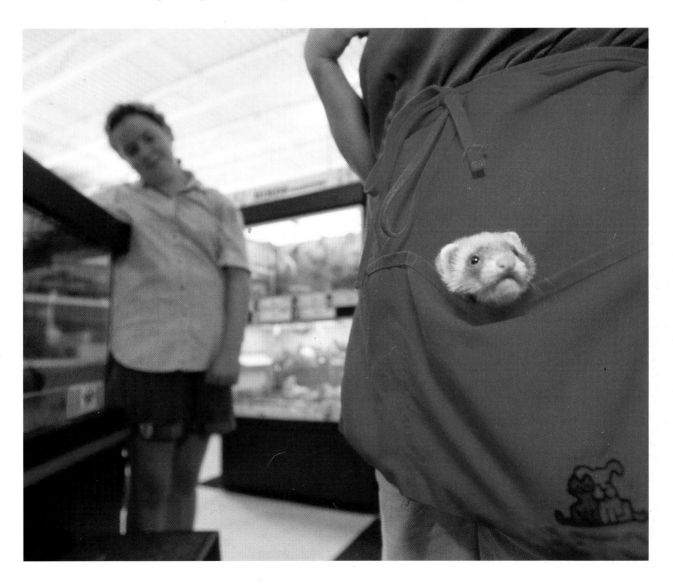

A pet store worker saw me looking at the ferrets for a long time. She took a ferret out of the cage and let me hold it. It climbed up my arm and sniffed my hair and nibbled my fingers. I could tell it was curious and wanted to play. It had the most adorable face. I decided right then that I wanted a ferret of my own. I talked about the ferret all the way home.

The best way to hold a ferret is to use one hand to hold its upper body and the other to support its hind end.

My mom is an animal lover just like I am. She liked the ferrets too. She wasn't ready to get a new pet just like that, though. She didn't know much about ferrets and wasn't sure they would fit into our household. What if cats like to eat ferrets, or the other way around? Mom had even heard that it was against the law to have pet ferrets in certain states and cities.

I can't believe it's against the law to have ferrets in some places!

I found out a lot about ferrets by using the Internet.

Mom called the Department of Fish and Wildlife to find out if it was okay to own ferrets in our town. They told her we could. I was so relieved! So Mom took me to the library to find out more about ferrets. We have a computer at home, and Mom said we could look on the World Wide Web for information too. After we knew more, we'd talk it over as a family. If we all agreed, we could go back to the pet store and buy one. My little sisters both got excited at the thought of getting a new pet. They'd never even seen a ferret! I was pretty excited too.

Striped Skunk

What Are Ferrets?

Ferrets are mustelids—members of the family Mustelidae, also known as the weasel family. Other mustelids are weasels, skunks, minks, and otters. Ferrets are also related to the black-footed ferret, an endangered wild animal that lives in the western United States. Many people think ferrets are rodents, like rats and guinea pigs. Rodents have teeth that keep growing, and they have to gnaw to keep their teeth from getting too long. Ferrets and other mustelids don't need to gnaw.

Short-tail Weasel

The polecat, found mainly in Europe, is the domestic ferret's closest relative. In fact, scientists can't agree about whether the ferret is a separate species (kind) of animal or simply a type of polecat. Whatever it may be, the domestic ferret is the only mustelid that is kept as a pet.

Ferrets come in many different colors and patterns. The most common color is sable. Sable ferrets have a brownish coat with darker brown markings. Albino ferrets have pure-white coats and red eyes. There is another kind of white ferret that has dark eyes. Other ferret colors include chocolate, silver, and cinnamon.

River Otter

Black-footed Ferret

The library had some books about keeping ferrets as pets. There was plenty of information on the Web, too. Mom, my sisters, and I learned a whole lot about ferrets in a short time. And the more I read, the more sure I was that ferrets are *great* pets.

Just like the ferret at the store, most ferrets are friendly, playful, and curious. They love to be with people. They aren't as affectionate as cats or dogs, but they're just as much fun. I also learned that most ferrets get along well with cats too. That made my mom and me feel much better. Mom was starting to like the whole idea of getting a ferret.

I read all the books I could find about ferrets. Taking notes helped me remember important facts about ferrets.

Well, it was more likely we would get two ferrets. It turns out that ferrets like each other's company. Many ferret owners have more than one ferret—sometimes *lots* more than one. Two ferrets would be more fun for them, and for us.

I was starting to feel like I had read everything ever written about ferrets. It was time to make a decision. One night about a week after the trip to the pet store, my whole family sat down and talked about the idea. Dad had lots of questions. He wasn't too sure about the idea of bringing more animals into our house. He and Mom both wanted to know how much it would cost to keep two ferrets. Good thing I had done my research!

We talked it over as a family before deciding to get two ferrets.

Even though they're small, ferrets can be expensive to have. It's not just the cost of getting the ferrets, which can be $100 or more for each ferret. Food and litter for two ferrets costs about $10 to $20 a month (depending on the brands). We also had to plan to spend about $150 for a cage, litter boxes, and toys. Taking the ferrets to the veterinarian would be another expense. Ferrets need shots and a checkup every year.

Ferrets love all kinds of tubes and balls. I couldn't wait to stock up on toys for my ferrets!

Ferrets need a cage, toys, food, and shots. Having ferrets costs about the same as having cats.

We weren't even sure we could find a vet. Not all vets take ferrets as patients. Luckily, my mom called our vet and found out that he would take care of our ferrets. He already had some ferret patients at his clinic. He told us that shots for a ferret cost about $50 to $75 per year. If a ferret gets sick and needs special care, it's more expensive.

It sounded like pet ferrets would be a little more expensive than cats. I had some money saved up from birthdays and Christmas. My parents said I could use some of it to buy the ferrets and some supplies. Since I was willing to do that, they said, they would take care of the rest.

Mom takes care of our llamas. She said she'd help me with the ferrets, but I would have to do most of the work. That was okay with me.

My parents wanted to make sure that I would be responsible for the ferrets. We talked about everything I'd need to do. Mom said she would help me when I needed it. Ferrets use litter boxes, like cats do, so they don't need to be walked. But their owners do have to feed them and keep their cages clean. And most important, you have to play with them for at least two hours a day! I didn't think it would be a big deal to be responsible for the ferrets. After all, I already helped take care of our cats.

I have a friend who babysits for a family with ferrets. They let me visit and ask them questions.

Mom and Dad didn't let me just leave it at that, though. They wanted to know how I would find time for ferret duty. I have a lot going on already, with play rehearsals and school and homework. So we worked out a ferret-care schedule. I would have to get up a few minutes earlier on weekdays to feed them and clean the cage. It would be worth it to have ferrets.

Finally, it was all settled. I was going to become a ferret owner! All I had to do was find the right ones for me.

We had to do some ferret-proofing . . .

Pet stores are just one of the ways to find pet ferrets.

There are a few different ways to find pet ferrets. One is to buy them at a pet store. Not all pet stores have ferrets, but larger ones like Petco usually do. Pet store ferrets have usually been neutered or spayed so that they can't have babies.

Usually pet store ferrets have also been "descented." That means the scent glands near their tails have been removed. This keeps them from being able to spray bad-smelling stuff like skunks do. Some people think it's unnecessary to descent a ferret. I wasn't sure what I thought about it.

You can also buy ferrets from a breeder. The American Ferret Association (AFA) has a list of breeders around the United States. Some breeders put ads in the newspaper or on a website. If you buy from a breeder, you may have to pay for descenting and spaying or neutering. That can cost around $100 to $200 each.

Spaying or neutering may be expensive, but it has to be done. Male ferrets (hobs) should be neutered by the age of six months. Otherwise they may become unfriendly and even attack other ferrets. Female ferrets (jills) must be spayed before they go into heat. This usually happens when they are about six months old. If they aren't spayed, and they don't mate, they can become sick and die.

Young ferrets are called kits. I can't believe how cute and tiny they are!

If you live in a town that has a ferret shelter, that's an especially good way to find a pet ferret. Shelters take in ferrets that have been given up by people who can't or don't want to take care of them. It also costs less to adopt from a shelter. You usually just have to pay a small fee to cover the cost of the ferret's shots. Some shelters even include the price of spaying or neutering in the adoption fee.

I called the ferret shelter myself to find out about available ferrets.

We wanted kits because we wanted to be sure that they were trained right and loved enough. Besides, kits are so adorable.

The shelter near us didn't have space to keep ferrets. Instead, they found foster homes for them. Foster ferret owners take care of ferrets until the shelter finds a permanent home for them. We visited two different foster homes. The first one had two adult ferrets. They were cute, and we liked them. But we wanted ferrets that were a little younger. Adult ferrets usually need less training than kits. But adults can be harder to train if their first owners didn't train them.

The second foster family had two six-month-old female ferrets. They were already litter-trained and spayed. They were also beautiful and very friendly. We knew right away that they were the ferrets for us.

Our ferret cage has three stories, so the ferrets have plenty of room for eating, sleeping, and playing.

I had a good time buying ferret supplies.

Before we brought our new pets home, we went shopping for some basic equipment. First, we bought a big cage with lots of room for playing. We also bought food, litter boxes, and dishes for their food and water.

Some pet stores put wood chips or shavings on the floor of ferret cages. It's not a good idea to do this at home. Ferrets can be allergic to the wood or shavings.

I did want to put something soft on the floor of the cage as a bed, though. The pet store had the perfect thing. It was a felt pouch, with stiff sides like a box. The ferrets could climb into it and snuggle up to sleep. Old T-shirts, sweatshirts, and towels work too. We also bought two hammocks to hang in the cage.

I hid wires that a ferret might want to play with— or chew on. Ferrets are so curious about everything. If they get up on a shelf, you can bet they'll knock everything off of it.

Ferrets love to hide, and they're really good at squeezing into small spaces. That means they can get into a lot of trouble in a house. So we didn't plan to let them be loose in the house when we weren't around. But we wanted to be able to play with them all over when we were home. That meant that we had to do some ferret-proofing.

First, we decided that the upstairs office would be off-limits to the ferrets. It's full of papers, computer equipment, and other important stuff that they could damage. Then we agreed to keep them in one room at a time, with the doors shut, whenever we played with them. I also had to clean my room. I hid books and papers away and put breakable things out of reach.

Next, we checked the house for cracks or holes wider than one square inch. Ferrets can squeeze into these tiny spaces and get lost or hurt. We decided to block up the fridge and the stove to make sure they couldn't get behind or under them. We put childproof latches on the kitchen cabinets. Then we closed drawers and closet doors all over the house. We did all this mostly for their safety, but also to protect our stuff.

Finally the house was ready for the ferrets. And so were we!

Our house was about to become a "Ferret Crossing" zone!

Dangers to Ferrets

Ferrets love to explore and hide. They are able to squeeze into small spaces, which can cause them to become lost, stuck, or hurt. Since you can't watch your ferrets every minute, you'll need to do some ferret-proofing to keep your pets safe.

Check your home for holes or cracks wider than 1 inch and find ways to block them up. Pay special attention to openings in and around these areas:

- walls and floors
- clothes dryers and washing machines
- furnaces
- kitchen and bathroom cabinets
- appliances such as refrigerators, stoves, and dishwashers

Here are some other ferret safety tips:

• Replace or patch torn window and door screens. Even a small hole may be big enough for a ferret to slip through.

• Warn visitors to check for ferrets before sitting down on a couch or chair. A favorite ferret hiding place is behind, between, or under couch cushions. Be especially careful with recliners and sofa beds.

• Keep small objects out of ferrets' reach. Ferrets like to hide small things, but they can also swallow them, which could block ferrets' intestines.

• Put lids on wastebaskets or make sure they are out of ferrets' reach.

• Keep sponges and soap away from ferrets. They like to chew on these things and may swallow pieces of them.

CHAPTER 3

Their names just seemed to suit them . . .

My ferrets rode home in our cat carrier—and got their names along the way.

On the way home, the ferrets rustled around in the cat carrier. We talked about what to name them. I wanted to get to know them before picking names. But in the car, I noticed that they were fascinated by some candy wrappers on the seat. When my sister Claire crinkled the wrappers, the ferrets stopped making noise and listened. They looked like they wanted to jump right out of the carrier. The wrappers gave me the ideas for the ferrets' names: Snickers and Skittles. Somehow those names just seemed to suit them.

My sisters were so excited to play with Snickers and Skittles.

When we got home, I let my sisters hold the ferrets for just a minute. Then Snickers and Skittles watched while Mom and I set up the cage. First, I put the ferrets' food and water dishes on one level. The dishes were far from the corner where the litter box would go. Ferrets are clean animals. They don't like to eat or sleep too close to their litter box. I filled the dishes with food and water. Ferrets like to eat and drink small amounts all day long. Their food and water dishes should always be full.

What to Feed a Ferret

Ferrets are carnivores. That means their diets must include meat, which is a good source of fat and protein. Many people feed their ferrets high-quality cat or kitten food. Brands such as Science Diet or Iams have all the nutrients ferrets need. So do most brands of food made just for ferrets. Ask your vet about a particular brand if you have any questions, or ask the vet to recommend a type of food.

Ferrets eat about five to seven small meals per day. Unless a ferret is overweight, its food dish should be kept full at all times. Most ferret owners like to give their pets treats occasionally. Ferrets love treats, so you have to be careful to not overdo it. "People food" treats should be given in very small amounts. It's best not to give more than one teaspoon per day.

Treats that are okay for your ferret:

Fruits
Vegetables
Bread
Peanut butter
Ferret treats from a pet store, such as Ferret Bites
Meat-flavored cat treats

Treats that you should *not* give your ferret:

Cheese, milk, ice cream, and other dairy products
Chocolate
Candy and other sweets
Salty foods
Onions
Garlic

I wanted to give the ferrets even more places to go inside their cage, and Mom helped me hang up the hammocks we had bought. I wondered if they would each take one hammock, or if they would both hang out in one together. Next, I set up the felt pouch that we had chosen as a bed. I tucked it into the corners of the cage. It started to look pretty cozy in there.

Mom and I set up the ferrets' cage. I'm glad my room is big enough for it.

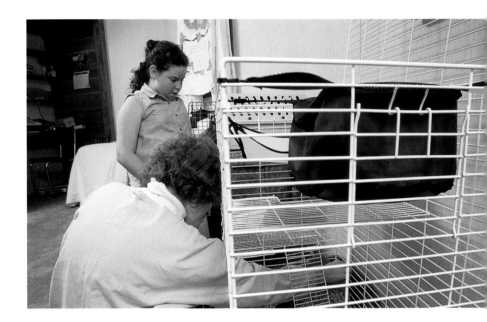

Mom helped me organize the cage. The litter boxes fit perfectly in the corners.

The last step before I could put Snickers and Skittles in their new home was the litter. We had gotten two regular-size cat litter boxes to use when the ferrets were loose in the house. We also bought two boxes that were designed for ferrets' cages. They're shaped like a triangle, to fit in the cage's corners. That's because ferrets like to poop and pee in corners. The front sides of the litter boxes are low to make it easy for the ferrets to climb in and out.

I filled both litter boxes with wood-stove pellets from the hardware store. It's cheaper than the special ferret litter that pet stores sell. Some people use pelletized newspaper, and others use flushable cat litter. The clumping type of cat litter is not good for ferrets.

My ferrets' foster "mom" told us that both Snickers and Skittles liked to dig in their litter box and kick litter around. I put in just a small amount so there wouldn't be as much to kick. Then, to be extra safe, we set the whole cage on top of a giant litter pan. If the ferrets knocked any litter out of their cage, it would fall into the big pan, not onto the carpet.

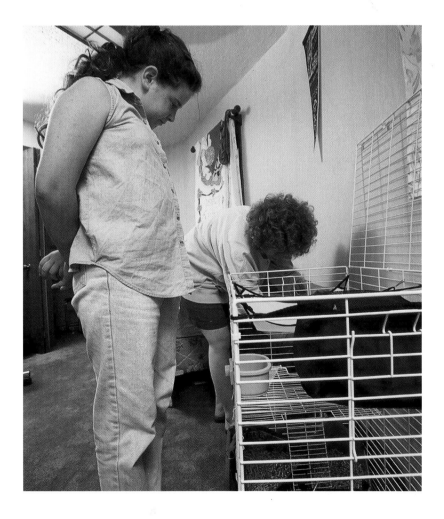

I thought putting a big litter pan underneath the cage was smart. I didn't want my carpet to get dirty.

Time for the ferrets to try out their new home!

Finally the cage was all ready. I put Snickers and Skittles into it. They seemed nervous at first and mostly just sniffed it. Pretty soon, though, they started to explore. They climbed and scrambled around. They tried out the hammocks and crawled into the pouch.

My sisters and I just watched them for a while. Then they nibbled at their food, and Snickers drank a little water. They seemed more interested in splashing around in their water dish, though. The whole bottom of the cage got wet. Luckily, we had bought a water bottle too. I filled that up and hung it on the side of the cage. Then I took out their water dish. Maybe we would try it again when they were older.

After dinner, Snickers tried out the litter box right away. Even though there wasn't that much litter in the box, she still kicked a lot of it around. I decided to take some litter out of both boxes. After that, it was Skittles's turn to use the box. She didn't make nearly as much of a mess.

I cleaned the litter box that night before bed and again the next morning. Ferrets don't like to use a dirty litter box. I also made sure they had food and fresh water before I left for school. So far, taking care of Snickers and Skittles was easy!

Before long, Skittles looked right at home in her cage.

The first few weeks were full of surprises . . .

My ferrets are full of energy.
They love to play with each
other—and with us.

We had learned a lot about ferrets. Still, the first few weeks with Snickers and Skittles were full of surprises. We were amazed by how much fun they were. They just loved to run around and play. They chased each other (and us), climbed all over each other (and us), and even groomed each other.

Getting to know my ferrets was fun!

We were happy to discover how much they seemed to like being around us. Ferrets are more like dogs than cats in that way—they love to be with people. And when they're happy, they hop around. It kind of looks like they're dancing, and it cracks me up. Some people call it the weasel war dance. They also make a funny little clucking noise. It's called "dooking," because it sounds like they're saying "dook dook dook" really fast. Snickers and Skittles always dook and dance when we take them out of their cage.

Their playfulness has its bad side too. We had read that ferrets could be sneaky. But we didn't know how sneaky, or how quick, they really are. One day the ferrets were playing in the living room. Snickers had disappeared under the couch— really disappeared. We couldn't see her or figure out where she was hiding.

Mom and I looked all over for her. Meanwhile, Skittles managed to escape into the kitchen. I chased her around for a few minutes. Then I finally grabbed her just as she was heading behind the refrigerator. (We hadn't blocked it up yet.) Just then, Snickers reappeared from behind the couch. We found out later that she had gotten into a hole in the lining underneath the couch. Don't ask me how we knew.

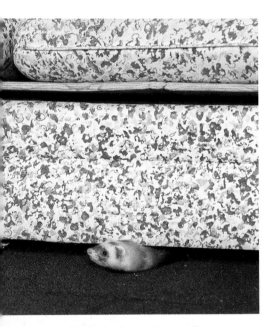

Ferrets love to explore every inch of a house and to find new hiding places.

I had to work on training Snickers not to nip. But she learned fast. Sometimes it's hard to make sure my toys don't become ferret toys!

At first, Skittles and Snickers (especially Snickers) also liked to nip. It didn't hurt that much, but it's not much fun either. We trained them not to nip by scruffing them and saying "No!" firmly every time they did it. Scruffing means picking them up by the skin around the back of the neck. It's how their mothers carry them when they're babies. It makes them relax and go limp. We also gave them a treat if they licked our fingers instead of biting them. After a few days, they got the idea and stopped biting.

Another ferret trick is stealing things and hiding them. Anything they can steal, they will. They even steal things that look too big for a ferret to carry. (My dad's shoes, for instance.) If you live with a ferret and you can't find your keys, chances are that the ferret took them.

At my house, we check chairs for ferrets before we sit down.

It took Snickers a few days to learn how to go up and down stairs.

Snickers and Skittles especially like to steal socks. My mom thinks that's good, because it makes us remember to put our socks away. If we forget, we won't see the socks again for days, or ever. It doesn't matter how many toys we give the ferrets. They love their toys, but they love socks even more.

We did notice that ferrets sometimes have trouble remembering to use a litter box when they need to poop or pee. We make sure there's a litter box in the room during playtime. It helps if we put some used litter from their cage in it. That makes it smell familiar. If we see them heading for a corner, we usually grab them and put them in the box. If we don't catch them in time, we clean the spot with soap and water right away. That keeps it from smelling like a place where they're supposed to poop or pee.

Ferret Facts

• Ferrets have lived with humans for at least 2,000 years—maybe even longer than people have kept cats as pets!

• For hundreds of years, hunters have trained ferrets to chase rabbits and other small animals. Ferrets are sent into rabbit holes and other hiding places. Then they flush out the animals so that the hunter can catch them. Using ferrets for hunting is known as "ferreting." Ferreting is still popular in Great Britain.

• Unlike cats and dogs, ferrets can catch colds and flus from humans. If anyone in your family has a cold or the flu, they should avoid touching the ferret until they feel better.

This British hunter uses ferrets to find rabbits.

• The average male ferret weighs 3-4 pounds. The average female ferret weighs 1-2 pounds.

• It's against the law to own a ferret anywhere in the states of California and Hawaii, and in New York City and Washington, D.C. Ferret lovers in those places are working to change the law.

• Leonardo da Vinci, the famous 15th-century artist and inventor, included ferrets in one of his paintings. More recently, a ferret starred in a TV commercial for Budweiser beer.

We found out pretty quickly that Snickers and Skittles will do almost anything for a treat. They really like the ferret treats that we get at the pet store. They also like cat food, peanut butter, crackers, and strawberries. But most of all, they love raisins. If one of the ferrets gets loose or disappears, I can always find her by shaking a box of raisins.

Snickers is crazy about raisins! She always comes out of hiding when she hears the box rattle.

Ferrets love Linatone, but you can't give them too much.

Snickers and Skittles have one other favorite treat. It's called Linatone. It must taste really good, because the ferrets will stand on their hind legs and beg for it. Linatone is a vitamin supplement. That means it's healthy and good for them. There's another vitamin treat called Ferretone, which is basically just like Linatone. Too much Linatone or Ferretone will make a ferret sick. We only give them a couple of drops at a time, every few days.

It was time for a checkup . . .

Snickers and Skittles seemed healthy, but they still needed a checkup.

Before long, it was time for Snickers and Skittles to have a checkup and get a couple of shots. We took them to see Dr. Cameron, our vet. One shot was for canine distemper. It's a disease that dogs get, and ferrets need to be protected from it too. The other shot was for rabies. The vet would also check them over to make sure they were healthy.

Everyone at the vet's office was really nice. They don't see too many ferrets, so they were interested in Snickers and Skittles. The ferrets seemed sort of nervous. They squirmed a lot, and Skittles trembled and held on to me really tight.

Dr. Cameron looked through their fur for fleas and checked their ears for ear mites. Ear mites are tiny bugs that make them itch. Dr. Cameron checked their teeth and gums. He looked under their tails. He listened to their hearts with a stethoscope, just like people doctors do. Then he gave them their shots. They weren't too happy about that!

Skittles didn't like it when Dr. Cameron looked in her ears, but she was a real trouper.

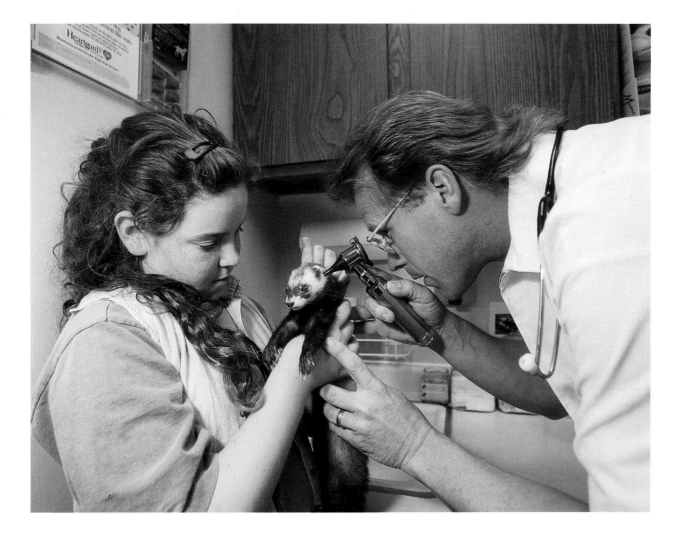

Dr. Cameron said that they both seemed perfectly healthy. Then he talked about things we needed to do to keep them healthy. We would need to cut their nails every few weeks and clean their ears if necessary. He said we should make sure they got enough exercise. Also, we should bring them in if we saw any signs of illness.

Dr. Cameron gave us tips on how to keep my ferrets healthy.

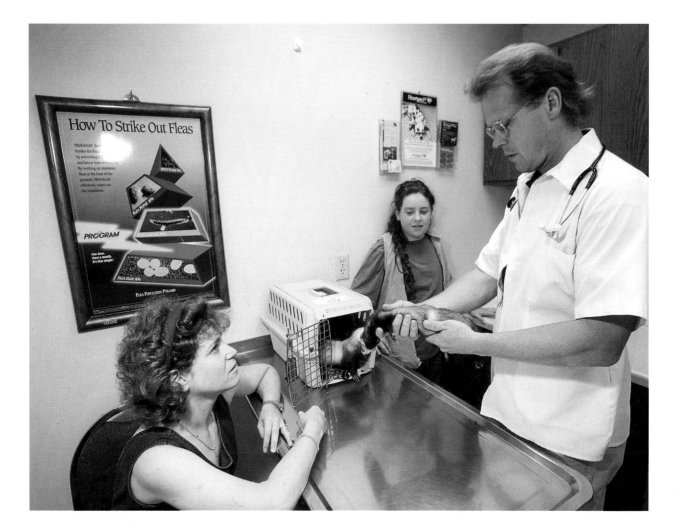

Ferret Health

Healthy ferrets are lively and alert. They have bright eyes and a full, soft, shiny coat of fur. It's important to spend time with your ferrets and become familiar with their normal behavior. That way, you'll notice any behavior changes or other signs of illness.

Below is a list of common signs of illness in ferrets. If your ferret shows any of these signs, call your veterinarian.

- lack of energy
- change in personality, such as becoming less active or more aggressive
- falling down or losing balance
- hair loss
- weight gain or loss
- lumps or bumps
- difficulty waking up
- lots of coughing or sneezing (some is normal)
- diarrhea
- vomiting
- not eating or drinking
- not pooping or peeing
- difficulty breathing
- green or yellow stool (poop)
- runny eyes
- runny nose
- scratching more than usual

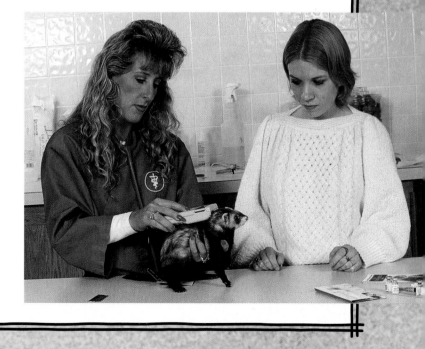

Dr. Cameron had said Snickers and Skittles would be tired from the shots, and they were. When we got home, we decided to give them a break for the rest of the day. We'd wait until the next day to cut their nails. They must have needed the break, because they slept for most of the evening. I told them that if they stayed healthy, they wouldn't have to go back to the vet for another year. I hope they understood.

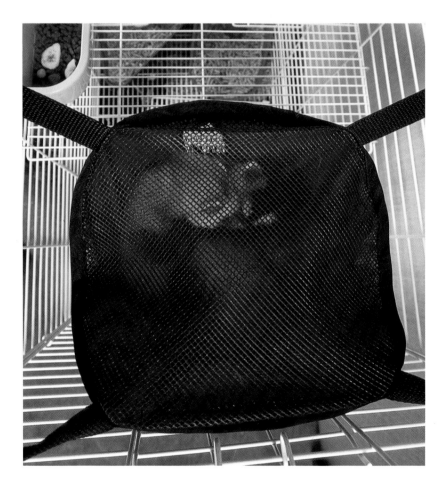

After their trip to the vet, the ferrets just wanted to sleep.

Skittles licks up the Linatone I put on her belly. We always cut the ferrets' nails in bright light so we can see the quick and avoid it.

Mom usually does most of the nail cutting. I help hold the ferrets because they can get pretty wriggly. We use a regular nail scissors, but small nail clippers work too. You have to be careful not to cut the nail down too far. If you do, you'll cut into the quick. That's a vein inside the nail. Cutting it will cause pain and make it bleed.

We figured out another way to make nail cutting time easier for everyone. We put a little bit of Linatone on their bellies. They get so interested in licking up every last drop of Linatone that they almost forget what you're doing to them.

I do what I can to make bathtime easy on my ferrets. Skittles usually tries to escape anyway.

Ferrets have a pretty strong smell, even if they have been descented. Keeping the cage and bedding clean is the best way to make sure their smell isn't a problem. We wash the ferrets' bedding about once a week. Bathing the ferrets also helps.

Bathing ferrets is a lot more fun than trimming their nails! First we put a little bit of warm (but not too warm) water and lots of toys in the tub. Then in go the ferrets. Skittles and Snickers don't exactly love being bathed. But they'll play and splash around for a while before they start trying to escape. We wash them with a little bit of special ferret shampoo. Then we rinse them very carefully to make sure all the shampoo is gone. Ferrets groom themselves by licking, and licking shampoo would give them a stomachache.

Along with bathing my ferrets, I wash their bedding once a week and clean their litter box every day.

When bathtime is over, I take the ferrets out one at a time. I rub them lightly in a towel and try to dry them as much as I can. Then I let them loose. They tear around the room like crazy. I don't know if they're trying to get totally dry or if they're just happy to be out of the bath.

We don't bathe the ferrets much in the winter unless they're extra dirty. It's too cold for them to run around wet, even with the heat on. Also, too many baths can dry out ferrets' skin and make them itchy. Some owners bathe their ferrets as often as twice a month. I don't think Snickers and Skittles would like that. But it's good to give them a bath every month or two. And they're so soft and fluffy afterwards!

They love to chase each other...

Ferrets and other pets should be introduced to each other gradually.

After another week or so, we were all used to living with Snickers and Skittles. All of us, that is, except for Jane and Michael, the cats. The ferrets and the cats were very curious about each other. We introduced them slowly. We started by letting the cats sniff our fingers after we'd been playing with the ferrets, and then the other way around.

After a while, we let them meet each other face to face. We watched all the animals carefully. At first, the cats looked at the ferrets like they were aliens from outer space. Jane hissed a few times. She even tried to scratch Skittles once. But they got used to each other after a while. Jane mostly ignores the ferrets these days. Michael likes them, though. He even joins in sometimes when I'm playing with Snickers and Skittles.

Over time, ferrets and cats can become good friends.

Ferrets and Other Pets

Most ferrets can get along with cats, dogs, and other ferrets. They are less likely to get along with pet rabbits, guinea pigs, hamsters, gerbils, and birds. With any pet, it's important to introduce new animals slowly and carefully. Here are some suggestions for introducing a ferret to another pet.

• Keep the pets in separate rooms.
• Start by leaving one pet loose while the other is in its cage or carrier. If the loose pet is a dog, keep it on a leash.
• Speak softly and gently to both animals. Pay lots of attention to both pets.
• If either pet tries to attack the other, separate the pets. Try again the next day. It may take days or even weeks for the animals to get used to each other.
• Once the pets have gotten used to each other while in the carrier, try letting both pets loose in one room. There should be another person in the room. One person should hold the ferret. The other can hold the cat or the dog's leash. Be prepared to separate the animals quickly if one attacks the other.
• Some dogs will see the ferret as something to chase and catch. If your dog does not learn to see the ferret as a pet, you will need to keep the dog on a leash whenever the ferret is loose.
• Never leave the pets alone together until you are absolutely sure that they get along.

Michael also sometimes tries to follow them into the ferret tube. It's just a long piece of dryer hose from the hardware store, but it's the best ferret toy ever. Plastic PVC pipe is a good toy too, but dryer hose is more fun. It's see-through, and you can watch the ferrets playing inside it. Snickers and Skittles love to chase each other into and out of the tube. It totally cracks me up.

You never know what might make a good ferret toy. Snickers and Skittles like playing in old pants legs that have been cut off. We have all kinds of other toys for them—little plastic toys, stuffed animals, and balls. They make other things into toys sometimes, like socks or an empty box. They also like any sort of bag that makes noise. But the tube is still their favorite.

Snickers and Skittles love running through tubes. When they get tired, they rest at an opening and peek out at me.

Sometimes it feels like Skittles is taking me for a walk! People we meet on our walks are usually curious about ferrets and ask me lots of questions.

I wanted to be able to take Snickers and Skittles outside. You can't let ferrets loose outdoors; it's too dangerous for them. So I trained them to walk on a leash. Regular neck collars don't work very well for ferrets. They can usually wriggle out of them. Special ferret harnesses work better. The tricky part is getting the harness onto the ferret! Mom sometimes has to help me. Once it's on, they don't seem to mind it.

Ferrets won't heel the way dogs do, but you can teach them to walk along with you. In fact, Snickers and Skittles get so excited about being outside that they usually walk ahead of me. They sniff and sniff and try to crawl under things. Keeping up with them is a workout!

I never get tired of making up new games to play with Snickers and Skittles. We play chase, catch, hide-and-seek (they always win that one!), slide-down-the-tube, climb-the-arm, and lots of other games that I don't even have names for. The ferrets play until they drop if I give them a chance. If I'm done playing but they're not, they jump around at my feet or try to climb up my pants leg.

I like looking for new toys whenever we go to the pet store too. I think I've already bought all the ferret toys they have there, but some cat toys work just as well. I always make sure the toy doesn't have eyes, buttons, or anything else that the ferrets could bite off and swallow.

Snickers likes trying to take a toy away from me. Skittles could hang out in her tube for hours.

Ferret shows are a good place to meet other ferrets and their owners.

Once in a while, I get the chance to show Snickers and Skittles to the world. There are ferret shows like the ones for dogs and cats, where the animals win prizes. We find out about shows from signs at the pet store and by talking to other ferret owners. Snickers and Skittles have each won prizes at shows. I keep their blue ribbons for them, of course. They'd probably just hide them somewhere! They seem to like going to shows. I think they love showing everyone how cute and funny they are.

Skittles looks so cute when she's sleeping. Maybe two ferrets aren't enough!

Sometimes after Snickers and Skittles have been playing for a couple of hours, they'll curl up in my lap and fall asleep. When they do, I let them stay that way for a while. Then I very carefully pick them up and put them back into their cage. They look so happy snuggled up together in a furry heap. But lately I've been thinking that the cage looks kind of empty with only two ferrets in it. I think it might be time to look for another ferret . . . or two . . . or more.

Glossary

Breeder: a person who raises animals to sell

Carnivores (*car*-nih-vorz): animals that eat meat. Dogs, cats, and ferrets are carnivores.

Descenting (dee-*sen*-ting): the removal of the scent glands near an animal's tail

Distemper (diss-*tem*-pur): a disease that is deadly to dogs, cats, and ferrets. Signs of distemper are fever, weakness, and not eating.

Ear mites: tiny bugs that can live inside some animals' ears. Ear mites are arachnids (uh-*rak*-nids), related to spiders.

Hob: a male ferret

Jill: a female ferret

Kit: a baby ferret

Mustelid (*muss*-tuh-lid): a member of the animal family Mustelidae, also known as the weasel family. Some mustelids are ferrets, weasels, minks, otters, and skunks.

Neuter (*noo*-ter): to remove the sex organs (testicles) from a male animal so that it is unable to reproduce

Nutrients (*noo*-tree-uhnts): the different substances in food that are needed by people, animals, and plants for good health

Rabies: a disease that affects the brain and spinal cord and can be deadly. Cats, dogs, ferrets, and people can get rabies.

Spay: to remove the sex organs (uterus and ovaries) from a female animal so that it is unable to reproduce

Resources

Organizations

American Ferret Association (AFA)
P. O. Box 255
Crownsville, MD 21032
http://www.ferret.org

International Federation of Ferret Breeders
P. O. Box 104
Maybee, MI 48159

**Shelters That Adopt and Rescue Ferrets
(STAR*Ferrets)**
P. O. Box 1714
Springfield, VA 22151-0714
http://www.netfopets.com/starferrets.html

Websites

Ferret Central
http://www.ferretcentral.org

The Ferret Owners' Manual
http://www.worldpath.net/~chip/fert-man.html

League of Independent Ferret Enthusiasts (LIFE)
http://www.acmeferret.com/life/

**The World Ferret Union/World Ferret
Information Centre**
http://home.worldonline.nl/~wfu/

The WWW Ferret Page
http://www.geocities.com/Heartland/Prairie/4282

For Further Reading

Bucsis, Gerry and Barbara Somerville. *Training Your Pet Ferret.* New York: Barrons, 1997.

Field, Mary. *Ferrets Today: A Complete and Up-to-Date Guide.* Philadelphia: Chelsea House, 1997.

Jeans, Deborah. *A Practical Guide to Ferret Care.* Miami, Fla.: Ferrets Inc., 1996.

Johnson, Sylvia A. *Ferrets.* (A Carolrhoda Nature Watch Book.) Minneapolis: Carolrhoda, 1997.

Shefferman, Mary. *The Ferret: An Owner's Guide to a Happy Healthy Pet.* New York: Howell Book House, 1996.

Siino, Betsy Sikora. *The Essential Ferret.* New York: Howell Book House, 1999.

Wallace, Bill. *Ferret in the Bedroom, Lizards in the Fridge.* New York: Pocket Books, 1989.

Winsted, Wendy. *Ferrets.* Neptune City, N.J.: T.F.H. Publications, 1995.

Index

ABOUT THE AUTHOR

Amy Gelman is an editor, writer, and translator. She loves animals and enjoys playing mandolin, singing, reading, and walking. She lives in Brooklyn, New York, with her family, which does not include any ferrets—yet.

ABOUT THE PHOTOGRAPHER

Andy King is a native of Boulder, Colorado, and graduate of Colorado State University. Andy has traveled around the world as a documentary and corporate photographer, and he has worked as a photographer at newspapers in Minnesota and Texas. He lives with his wife, Patricia, and their daughter in St. Paul, Minnesota, where he enjoys mountain biking and playing basketball.

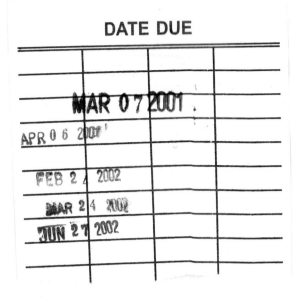